Managing Our Resources

Minerals
A resource our world depends on

Heinemann Library
Chicago, Illinois

Ian Graham

© 2005 Heinemann Library

a division of Reed Elsevier Inc.

Chicago, Illinois

Customer Service 888-454-2279

Visit our website at
www.heinemannlibrary.com

Designed by David Poole and
Paul Myerscough
Photo research by Melissa Allison and
Andrea Sadler

Originated by Ambassador Litho Ltd.
Printed in China by WKT Company Limited

09 08 07 06 05

10 9 8 7 6 5 4 3 2 1

**Library of Congress Cataloging-in-
Publication Data**
Graham, Ian, 1953-
    Minerals : a resource our world depends on
/ Ian Graham.
        p. cm. -- (Managing our resources)
    Includes bibliographical references and
index.
    ISBN 1-4034-5616-X (lib. bdg.) --
    ISBN 1-4034-5624-0 (pbk.)
    1. Mines and mineral resources--Juvenile
literature. I. Title.
    TN148.G7 2005
    549--dc22

                    2004005836

JJ 549

Acknowledgments
The author and publisher are grateful to the
following for permission to reproduce
copyright material: p. 4 W. Broadhurst/FLPA;
p. 5 top Papilio Neil Miller/Ecoscene; pp. 5
bottom, 21 Tom Bean/Corbis; p. 6 Jurgen &
Christine Johns/FLPA; p. 7 top Jeremy
Walker/Science Photo Library; p. 7 bottom
Tony Page/Ecoscene; p. 8 Sidney
Moulds/Science Photo Library; p. 9 top
Anthony Cooper/Ecoscene; p. 9 bottom
Photodisc/Getty Images; p. 10 Hans Dieter
Brandl/FLPA; p. 11 Catherine Mullen/FLPA;
p. 12 Joel Creed/Ecoscene; p. 13 top D.
Hall/FLPA; p. 13 bottom Mary Evans Picture
Library; p. 14 Alex Barter/Science Photo
Library; p. 15 Herman Eisenbess/Science
Photo Library; p. 16 J. Watkins/FLPA; p. 17
Topham Picturepoint ; p. 18 Geoff
Tompkinson/Science Photo Library; p. 19
Stephen Dalton/NHPA; p. 20 bottom D.
Warren/FLPA; p. 20 top Simon Fraser/Science
Photo Library; pp. 22 inset, 23 Science Photo
Library; p. 24 Alan Towse/Ecoscene; p. 25
Andrew Brown/Ecoscene; p. 26 Maurice
Nimmo/FLPA; p. 27 top Simon
Grove/Ecoscene; p. 27 bottom Michael
Pole/Corbis; p. 28 Andy Hibbert/Ecoscene; p.
29 Royal Botanical Gardens, Kew;

Cover photograph: First Light/Corbis.

Contents

Some words are shown in bold, **like this.** You can find out what they mean by looking in the glossary.

What Are Minerals?

Minerals are natural resources that are found in the ground. Rocks are made of minerals. All minerals are made of **crystals,** like grains of salt pressed together. Some minerals, such as quartz and diamonds, sparkle, while many others look like rock or soil.

Most minerals are made from two or more substances combined. Many minerals contain a metal. Some of the metals found in minerals are also found in the ground, separate from any other substances. These metals are minerals, too. They include gold, silver, copper, and tin.

How are minerals formed?

Some minerals are formed when **molten** rock cools down and becomes solid. As the rock cools, mineral crystals form in it. These are called primary minerals. Quartz and feldspar are examples of primary minerals. Other minerals are formed later, when rock is changed, perhaps by great heat or pressure, or by the effect of weather.

All metals and **gemstones** are found in **mines** or **quarries.**

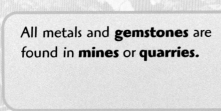

These minerals are called secondary minerals. Kaolinite, a mineral found in china clay, is an example of a secondary mineral.

Are minerals useful?

Minerals are very useful. Many minerals contain metals and other substances that are used to make things. Rocks that contain the most useful minerals are also called **ores**. A metal called aluminum comes from an ore called bauxite. Lots of other ores have names that end with -*ite* as well.

Bauxite is mined because it contains the metal aluminum.

Did you know?

Coal, oil, and natural gas are not minerals because they come from living things. Even so, they are often called minerals or mineral fuels because they are useful materials that are **extracted** from the ground.

What Are Minerals Used For?

Almost everything around you contains minerals or materials that come from minerals. The latest electronic gadgets, airliners, cars, and skyscrapers could not be made without minerals.

How are minerals used in buildings?

Big buildings start off with a steel frame. Steel is made from iron, a metal that comes from minerals such as hematite. The floors are made from concrete, which is made from limestone, a rock that contains minerals such as calcite and dolomite. Water is carried around the building inside pipes made from copper, which comes from minerals such as cuprite. The windows are made from glass, which is made from minerals that contain **silica**.

How do fireworks use minerals?

Minerals make fireworks noisy and colorful. Aluminum powder produces the flashes and bangs. Iron filings help to make golden sparks.

Ships are made from iron and steel, which come from minerals.

Copper makes blue colors, barium makes green, sodium makes yellow, and strontium makes red.

How are minerals used in jewelry?

Some of the most beautiful minerals are **gemstones,** which are used to make jewelry. They are **crystals** that form in rocks underground where the crushing weight of rock above and very high temperatures change the rocks. These minerals include diamonds, rubies, sapphires, emeralds, opals, and garnets.

Minerals give fireworks their bright colors.

Did you know?

Some minerals are not what they seem. A mineral called pyrite is often mistaken for gold. Because of this, it is also known as fool's gold.

The most expensive jewelry is made from mineral gemstones such as diamonds and rubies. This ruby is worth about $15 million.

What amount of minerals do we use?

People use minerals to generate electricity, heat houses, and build many things. On average, each person uses the following amounts of minerals during his or her lifetime:

- about 40 grams (1.5 ounces) of gold
- 925 pounds (420 kilograms) of lead
- 837 pounds (380 kilograms) of zinc
- 1,610 pounds (730 kilograms) of copper
- 1.6 tons of aluminum
- 10 tons of clay
- 13 tons of salt
- 15 tons of iron
- 770 tons of rock, stone, sand, gravel, and cement
- 22.5 tons of other minerals and metals.

Do living things need minerals?

Minerals are needed by plants and animals for growth and good health. The water plants draw up from the soil contains **dissolved** minerals. Animals get minerals by eating plants or other animals.

Minerals are used to provide many of the things you will need in your lifetime, such as metal to make cars and materials used to build houses.

The human body contains up to about 6.5 pounds (3 kilograms) of minerals. You need the right amounts of about twenty minerals to stay healthy. The most important minerals our food gives us are calcium, phosphorus, magnesium, iron, iodine, sodium, potassium, and zinc.

What do minerals do in your body?

Calcium, magnesium, and phosphorus strengthen your bones and teeth. Sodium and potassium help your body's cells to work properly. Iron helps the blood to collect oxygen from your lungs and carry it around your body.

We get the minerals our body needs from the things we eat and drink.

Did you know?

Your body can actually make tiny amounts of a few minerals. One of them, called hydroxylapatite, is found in your bones and teeth.

CASE STUDY:
Sears Tower, Chicago

Sears Tower in Chicago, Illinois, was the tallest building in the world when it opened in 1973. It stands 1,453 feet (443 meters) tall and weighs more than 202,000 tons. The tower's framework was built from 77,000 tons of steel— enough to build 50,000 cars. It also contains enough concrete to build an eight-lane highway 5 miles (8 kilometers) long.

The building's 110 floors, where 11,000 people work, are connected by about 43,000 miles (70,000 kilometers) of copper telephone cable— enough to go around the world 1.75 times. The building's outside is covered with aluminum, and the windows are tinted with bronze metal. All of these materials came from minerals.

Sears Tower in Chicago, Illinois, contains millions of pounds of materials made from minerals.

Where Are Minerals Found?

If you dig a deep enough hole in the ground, you will always find rock at the bottom. There is rock everywhere under the ground. This is Earth's **crust**. Rock is made from minerals, so minerals are found all over the world.

Are all minerals found everywhere?

Minerals are not spread evenly everywhere. Some minerals are found concentrated in pockets or layers. A layer of one mineral running through rock is called a seam.

The most common mineral in Earth's crust is feldspar. The next most common is quartz. Minerals containing precious metals such as gold, silver, and platinum are very valuable because they are rare and hard to find. Only about 195,000 tons of gold and 1.7 million tons of silver have been found in recorded history.

Rock sometimes forms in layers called strata. A layer of rock that is especially rich in one or more minerals is also called a seam.

How many minerals are there?

There are more than 3,000 different minerals. Only about 100 of them make up most of the rocks on Earth. Most of the rocks on Earth are made up of only eight **elements**—oxygen, silicon, aluminum, iron, calcium, sodium, potassium, and magnesium.

Are there minerals under the sea?

Minerals are found everywhere in the Earth's **crust**—under the land and under the sea. Minerals also come from the sea itself. Seawater contains bromine, lithium, boron, and magnesium. Salt is made by heating seawater to boil off the water and leave the salt behind. Minerals are also found on the seabed. Large areas of the seabed are covered with little lumps, called nodules. These contain a metal called manganese.

Most sand is made from **silica,** which contains the elements silicon and oxygen.

How Are Minerals Found?

The search for minerals begins with photographs of the ground taken from **satellites** in space and aircraft. **Geologists** use these photographs to draw maps of the different types of rocks on Earth's surface. The maps give clues about where certain minerals might be found. Small patches of one type of rock might mean there is more of the same rock, and the minerals it contains, underground. Geologists also try to figure out how the land formed. This can give clues about which minerals the rock there might contain.

As well as looking at the rocks and testing them, there are ways of finding some minerals by using magnets, **gravity,** electricity, and radiation.

Photographs taken from a satellite show large areas of land at once.

Magnetism

Some minerals are magnetic. If they are located at or near the ground surface, instruments called magnetometers can detect their magnetism and show where they are.

Gravity

A large amount of a very heavy mineral can make Earth's **gravity** stronger around where the mineral is located. Instruments that measure the strength of gravity can be used to find these minerals.

Electricity

Electricity flows better through some minerals than others. Measuring how well electricity flows through the ground gives **geologists** information about which minerals may lie underground.

Radiation

Some minerals give off **radioactive particles** of energy. Scientists use instruments that detect radioactivity to find these minerals.

Geologists test rocks to find out which minerals they contain.

How Are Minerals Extracted?

Minerals are **extracted** from the ground by digging them out. Digging for minerals is also called **mining**. If minerals are near the surface, the ground above them is scraped away and a shallow pit is dug to reach them. This is called open-pit mining. Minerals deeper underground are reached by digging shafts, or tunnels, down to them.

How are minerals dug out?

Some mineral-bearing rock can be dug out of the ground using a mechanical shovel. If the rock is very hard, explosions are used to break it into pieces before it is dug out. The machines used in mining are some of the biggest in the world. There are giant mechanical shovels that can scoop up tons of rock at a time. The shovels then load enormous trucks that can carry up to 363 tons of rock each.

Rock is shattered using explosions to make it easier to dig out.

What is panning?

It is possible to find gold without having to dig it out of the ground. If a river cuts through rock that contains gold, the water may wash out some of the gold. The heavy gold sinks to the bottom of the river. It can be found by panning. Water is swirled around a shallow pan with some river sand in it. The lighter sand is washed out while the heavy gold stays in the pan. Panning was a popular way of finding gold in the 1800s, but it is rarely used today because it only produces very small amounts of gold.

This gold miner was photographed panning for gold in California in 1890.

Did you know?

One of the world's deepest mines is the Western Deep Levels Gold Mine in South Africa. The deepest part is more than 11,745 feet (3,580 meters) below the ground. There are plans to dig 3 miles (5 kilometers) below the ground. This will be known as the Western Ultra Deep Levels.

What are the problems of deep mining?

Deep **mining** is very dangerous. Deep mines are hot and stuffy, and the mines sometimes collapse. The mines have to be fitted with electric lights so that the miners can see to work. Air has to be pumped down the mine so that the miners can breathe.

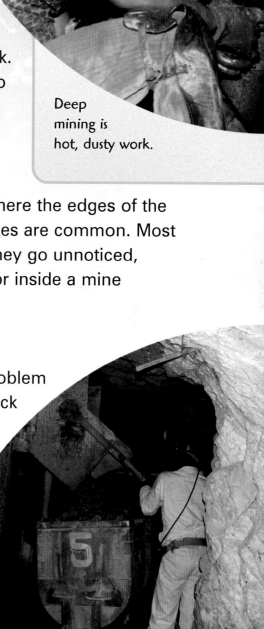

Deep mining is hot, dusty work.

Shifting ground

Earth's surface is made from plates of rock that move very slowly. In places where the edges of the plates rub against each other, earthquakes are common. Most of these movements are so small that they go unnoticed, but any movement of the ground near or inside a mine is dangerous.

Bursting rocks

The deepest mines can suffer from a problem called rock burst. The huge weight of rock above pressing down can squeeze the rock at the bottom of the mine so hard that pieces fly out of the mine's walls.

As the miners cut into rock, the roof of the roof has to be propped up to stop the mine from collapsing.

17

Hot rocks

The center of Earth is very hot, so the deeper a **mine** is, the hotter it is. At a depth of nearly 2.5 miles (4 kilometers), the rock is at a temperature of more than 140 °F (60 °C). It is impossible for **miners** to work in such a hot place, so the mine has to be cooled. Cooling down a mine is very expensive, so the deepest mines are dug for only the most valuable minerals, such as gold.

Did you know?

The center of Earth is made from iron, nickel, and other valuable metals, but it cannot be mined because it is as hot as the surface of the Sun—10,832 °F (6,000 °C). You would also have to dig a mine more than 3,900 miles (6,300 kilometers) deep to reach it!

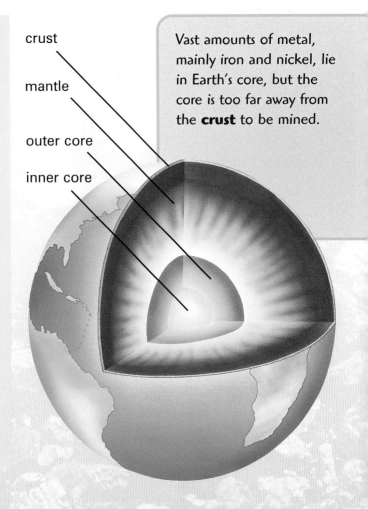

crust

mantle

outer core

inner core

Vast amounts of metal, mainly iron and nickel, lie in Earth's core, but the core is too far away from the **crust** to be mined.

CASE STUDY:
Bingham Canyon Copper Mine

The Bingham Canyon copper **mine** near Salt Lake City, Utah, is one of the biggest holes ever dug in the ground. It measures 2.5 miles (4 kilometers) across and more than half a mile (one kilometer) deep.

Mining began there in the 1860s, when people found lead, zinc, gold, and silver **ores** there. Altogether, the mine produces about 300,000 tons of copper, 100 tons of silver, and 14 tons of gold every year.

The Bingham Canyon mine has been producing copper and other metals for about 140 years.

How Are Minerals Processed?

Rock is **processed** to separate the most useful minerals from the rest of the rock. The processes used are crushing and grinding. Then the minerals are processed to **extract** useful materials from them. The processes used to do this are smelting and refining.

Why is the rock crushed first?

Crushing the rock produces a fine powder that is easier to separate into useful minerals and waste rock. Trucks bring the rock to machines that crush the rock. They break the big chunks of rock into smaller pieces. Then the smaller pieces are ground to a powder by tumbling them around together with hundreds of steel balls inside spinning drums. These ball mills produce a powder like very fine sand.

Rock is crushed to a powder to separate the minerals it contains.

How are the minerals separated?

Some minerals are heavier than others. Letting the powdered rock slide across shaking tables can make heavier minerals slide off in one direction while the lighter waste rock goes off in another direction. This is called **gravity** separation. Some minerals are magnetic, so they can be picked out by magnets.

Some minerals and the metals they contain are magnetic. For example, a magnet can be used to pick up a pile of iron filings.

How is water used in mineral processing?

Powdered rock is mixed with water and then air is blown through the water to make bubbles. Some of the minerals stick to the bubbles and float to the surface, where they are skimmed off. This is called flotation separation.

Did you know?

Magnetic iron **ore** is also called lodestone.

What is smelting?

Once the minerals have been separated, the next step is to **extract** useful materials from them. Metals are extracted from **ores** by smelting. An ore is heated to a high temperature in a furnace. Other materials added in the furnace combine with the ore. They are chosen so that they split up the ore into a metal and a waste material called slag. The **molten** metal runs out of the furnace.

How is iron smelted?

Iron ore contains iron and oxygen. Iron is extracted from the ore by heating the ore to 2,912 °F (1,600 °C) with limestone and charcoal or coke (a kind of charcoal made from coal). Iron made in this way is called pig iron.

Minerals are smelted in a furnace to extract the metals they contain.

Why is iron made into steel?

Pig iron is not pure iron. It contains carbon, which makes the iron break easily. Pig iron is made stronger by taking out some of the carbon. Oxygen is blown through molten pig iron in a furnace. The oxygen combines with carbon in the pig iron and makes gases. The gases bubble out, taking the carbon with them. Metal produced in this way is called steel.

Steel that is rolled into sheets can be used to make cars and ships.

A metal combined with another metal, or carbon, is called an alloy. Steel is an alloy of iron and carbon. Brass is an alloy of copper and zinc. Bronze is an alloy of copper and tin.

How are gemstones processed?

Natural **gemstones** look like pieces of dull glass. They are processed by cutting and grinding. First, they are cut into smaller gemstones with better shapes. Then flat areas called facets are made all over each stone. The facets act as mirrors, reflecting light. They give a cut gemstone its sparkle.

A well-cut diamond sparkles brightly.

CASE STUDY:
The Cullinan Diamond

The world's biggest diamond was found in South Africa in 1905. It was named after Sir Thomas Cullinan, the mine's owner. Diamonds are weighed in carats. A carat is equal to 0.007 ounces (0.2 grams). The Cullinan diamond weighed 3,106 carats, or about 22 ounces (620 grams). It was given to the British king, Edward VII. It was then cut into more than 100 diamonds. The biggest is the Star of Africa, or Cullinan I. This became part of the royal scepter in the British Crown Jewels. The second-largest diamond, called Cullinan II or the Second Star of Africa, was set in the British Imperial State Crown.

The biggest diamond in the British royal scepter is the Star of Africa, which was cut from the Cullinan diamond.

Did you know?

The *Koh-i-noor* (a Persian phrase meaning "mountain of light") diamond was owned by the emperors of India in the 14th century. It was presented to Queen Victoria in 1850. Later, it was set in the crown worn by King George VI's queen at a coronation in 1937.

How Are Minerals Transported?

Minerals have to be transported from where they are found to where they are **processed**. Then, the metals **extracted** from the minerals are transported all over the world to be made into things. Most minerals and metals are heavy and they usually need to be transported in large quantities. Big, powerful vehicles are needed to move them.

Which vehicles transport minerals?

Minerals are transported mainly by trucks, trains, and ships. Only the most precious metals and **gemstones,** such as gold and diamonds, are valuable enough to transport by air.

Did you know?

About 50 billion tons of **ore** are mined every year and have to be transported. That is enough rock to fill a hole that is about 3 feet (1 meter) deep and the size of Switzerland.

Ore carrier ships like the ones here are also called bulk carriers.

CASE STUDY:
A Huge Dump Truck

The Liebherr T282 dump truck is one of the biggest trucks in the world. It is used to haul as much rock as possible as fast as possible out of **mines** and **quarries**.

It is about four times the length and five times the width of a family car. It is so big that it has to be taken to the place where it is needed in pieces and built there. Even when it is empty, the Liebherr T282 weighs more than 200 tons. With a full load of rock on board, it can weigh more than 540 tons.

The Liebherr T282 dump truck is so big that the driver has to climb up a ladder to get into the cab.

How Can Minerals Affect the Environment?

Extracting minerals from the ground can damage the environment. Open-pit mines scar the landscape. **Mining** and mineral **processing** can create huge amounts of waste materials. Water running through mining locations and near waste piles can pollute nearby rivers and lakes. The waste materials produced when minerals are processed can also be dangerous to plants and animals.

Are some minerals more dangerous than others?

The most dangerous minerals are those that are **radioactive**. Just being near a radioactive **element** can be dangerous. Radiation can kill living cells or damage them. If cells that produce babies are damaged, newborn babies can be harmed.

Waste rock and soil from mining operations is often left in huge piles.

CASE STUDY: Chernobyl, 1986

The worst **radiation** accident in history happened near the city of Chernobyl in Ukraine in 1986, when part of a **nuclear power plant** exploded. The explosion caused radioactive **particles** to be released into the air. They were carried away by the wind and blew across several countries. Thousands of people who lived close to the power plant had to leave their homes. About 30 people died at the time of the explosion. At least another 8,000 people have died since then from illnesses caused by the radiation. Some farm animals more than 1,860 miles (3,000 kilometers) away were affected by radioactive particles from Chernobyl. The particles had been blown by the wind and landed on the grass they ate. This meant the animals themselves became too radioactive for people to eat.

The damaged part of the Chernobyl power plant was covered with concrete to stop more radiation from escaping.

Will Minerals Ever Run Out?

Nearly all the minerals we use today come from the top 3,300 feet (1,000 meters) of Earth's **crust**. If these minerals begin to run out, **geologists** will explore the next 3,300 feet (1,000 meters), and then the next layer. Earth's crust is about 43 miles (70 kilometers) thick, so they have much room left to explore. However, the deeper they have to go to find minerals, the more expensive it is to **mine** them. We can make minerals we are mining now last longer by **recycling** them.

Where else could minerals come from?

So far, there has been very little mining underneath the sea. This may be done in the future, although it could have a huge effect on the environment and habitats. In the future, if minerals are in very short supply, it could be worth mining them on the Moon and bringing them back to Earth.

In the future, some of our minerals might come from the Moon.

Glossary

crust rock that forms the surface of Earth

crystal material made from particles that form patterns. These patterns repeat themselves over and over again, making shapes with flat surfaces.

dissolved finely broken up within a liquid

element substance that cannot be split up into simpler substances. About 93 elements are found in nature and others have been made by scientists. Elements are made from particles called atoms.

extract take something out of something else, such as coal out of a field

gemstone mineral that is highly valued, because it is so beautiful and rare. Gemstones include diamonds, rubies, and sapphires.

geologist scientist who studies rocks and minerals

gravity force that pulls everything toward Earth. Everything has its own force of gravity, but large objects such as stars, planets, and moons have stronger forces of gravity because they are so big.

mining digging into the ground to reach valuable materials, such as coal. A person who mines is called a miner.

molten melted form

nuclear power plant building where electricity is made using energy from atoms, which are the smallest particles of an element. When uranium atoms are split apart inside a nuclear power plant, they give out heat that is used to change water into steam. The steam drives machines, called generators, that make electricity.

ore mineral from which a metal, or metals, can be extracted

particle very small bit of something

process to change a material by a series of actions or treatments

quarry hole in the ground where building materials such as stone or gravel are dug out

radioactive giving out rays of energy or particles by the breaking apart of atoms of certain elements, such as uranium

recycle to process for reuse instead of using materials only once and then throwing them away

satellite small object that orbits around a larger object, such as a spacecraft going around Earth

silica substance containing silicon and oxygen joined together that found in many rocks and minerals; also called silicon dioxide

More Books to Read

Edwards, Ron, and Lisa Dickie. *Diamonds and Gemstones.* New York: Crabtree Publishing, 2004.

Edwards, Ron, and James Gladstone. *Gold.* New York: Crabtree Publishing, 2004.

Prokos, Anna. *Rocks and Minerals.* Milwaukee, Wis.: Gareth Stevens, 2004.

Snedden, Robert. *Earth and Beyond.* Chicago: Heinemann Library, 1999.

Stewart, Melissa. *Minerals.* Chicago: Heinemann Library, 2002.

Trueit, Trudi Strain. *Rocks, Gems, and Minerals.* Danbury, Conn.: Scholastic Library, 2003.

West, Krista. *Hands-On Projects about Rocks, Minerals and Fossils.* New York: Rosen Publishing Group, 2002.

Whyman, Kathryn. *Rocks and Minerals and the Environment.* Mankato, Minn.: Stargazer Books, 2004.

Index